Not for me
and
Who was this?

Hannie Truijens

Illustrated by Annabel Spenceley

Not for me page 2

Who was this? page 9

HELEN MARRON
BOOKMARK
☎ 01213130256

Nelson

Not for me

"Who will come out to play with us?" said Helen and Adam.
"I will," said Mum.

"This is great," said Helen.

"Not for me," said Mum.

"This is great," said Adam.

"Not for me," said Mum.

"Down we go," said Helen.

"Look out, Mum."

"Here we come," said Adam.
"Look out, Mum."

"This is great," they all said.

"Not for me," said Mum.

"It was great, Dad," said Adam and Helen.

"Not for me," said Mum.

Who was this?

"Who was this?" said Adam.

"Let me have a look."

"Let me see your shoe, Grandad.
I think it was you.
No, your shoe is too big."

"Let me see your shoe, Dad.
I think it was you.
No, your shoe is too big."

"Let me see your shoe, Mum.
I think it was you.
No, your shoe is too big."

"Let me see your shoe, Tom.
I think it was you.
No, your shoe is too big."

"Let me see your shoe, Helen.
I think it was you.
No, your shoe is too small."

"Let me see your shoe, Adam," said Helen.
"I think it was you."

"Oh no," said Adam.

"Oh yes," said Grandad, Dad, Mum, Tom and Helen.